T0118304

To Touch The White Unfolded Wings Of Wonder

To Touch The White Unfolded Wings Of Wonder

Poetry By Chuck Rice

iUniverse, Inc.
New York   Bloomington

To Touch The White Unfolded Wings Of Wonder
Poetry By Chuck Rice

Copyright © 2009 by Chuck Rice

All rights reserved. No part of this book may be used or reproduced by any means, graphic, electronic, or mechanical, including photocopying, recording, taping or by any information storage retrieval system without the written permission of the publisher except in the case of brief quotations embodied in critical articles and reviews.

iUniverse books may be ordered through booksellers or by contacting:

iUniverse
1663 Liberty Drive
Bloomington, IN 47403
www.iuniverse.com
1-800-Authors (1-800-288-4677)

Because of the dynamic nature of the Internet, any Web addresses or links contained in this book may have changed since publication and may no longer be valid. The views expressed in this work are solely those of the author and do not necessarily reflect the views of the publisher, and the publisher hereby disclaims any responsibility for them.

ISBN: 978-1-4401-3604-7 (pbk)
ISBN: 978-1-4401-3605-4 (ebk)

Printed in the United States of America

iUniverse rev. date: 4/7/2009

To my wife Tracy
my most valuable critic
who loves me enough
to tell me the truth
and to Mark, friend
and fellow poet
who saw this
from the beginning.

Contents

Introduction

Poetry is a whale sighting! We live along the edges of this wondrous hidden world, a vast plane of existence in which most of us see very little of what lies beneath the surface. Its cadence conjures an adventurous sense of discovery that calls to someplace deep inside us. In a rare surging moment the elusive phantom breaks the dark surface of everything that separates us. At once we see its immense significance and intricate beauty. It majestically spouts a dazzling stream high over our heads. For a moment we see ourselves reflected in its gentle eye, united in common experience. Then with a grand splash it disappears back into the cold depths from which it came and we are left with but the mist of inspiration.

Firewood

Two Tibetan women lean,
framed against firewood
piled heads high
sectioned quartered and stacked
like pieces of time. Rings
that tell of killing
winters and burning summers
halo their hard lined faces,
weathered sides of mountains
breached with crevices of deep
smiles purified in pain
on lipless mouths, the withered
over-ripened fruit of hardship,
old women
that know desire
as reason
is the hunger of fire,
a bottomless hot thirst.

Near, their ashen
hand-washed dresses
hang flat
angling from taut
wind-cocked clotheslines,
clinging limbless ghosts
of wind being sucked
into oblivion.

Against the winter of life
we stack our logs of experience,
store cut-up wisdom
from increment to increment,
yet burn all knowledge
in each moment
surviving to the next.
Time becomes then
the poverty of existence
possessing only now-
the ever present moment
turning on its axis
like a multifaceted diamond
reflecting the faces of being
against the firelight
of reason and desire.

Original Scent

There are memories
encoded
in scents and smells,
embedded deeper
than the sticks
of words
can fathom.

At rare, random moments
one is triggered
and we are at once displaced,
the way death displaces,
left alone
in the great corridor
of time
without language,
feeling our way.

Perhaps connected,
all such memories
reach back
to the Garden itself,
to the first whet
luring scent
of forbidden fruit,
to the very moment
when we were willing
to risk all
for knowledge
and experience,
to wager beauty
that we might own pain.

The Spot

The raising of my right arm
for another sip of coffee
readjusts the kitchen light
across the cluttered surface
of the breakfast table
as I casually read
the morning paper.

I notice a faint grease spot,
perhaps virgin olive oil
for salad, smudged
by an unsuspecting forearm.
It is a small uncharted continent
in a tranquil sea of flowing
waves of maple grain.

Upon closer examination,
testing the various angles of light,
I discover a myriad maze
of tiny scratch lines in the wood,
entangled and overlapping
as the stories behind them,
each wanting to touch the other,
as I, at night, in our bed,
though taking comfort
in my separate side, want somehow
to touch, even with just my foot,
some part of my wife.

Are these the life-lines of the table,
like those in the palm of a hand?
Or more certain, its unique
and individual acquired fingerprint?
Perhaps we imprint the objects around us
with singular identities through our daily
contact, both purposeful and accidental,
continually changing identities,
much like the scars that help to define us.
It is not then the minted, unmarred beauty
of a thing that sets its value,
but the rare character
instilled by its wounds.

Faces

I want to travel
somewhere beyond the painful
barriers of my fears.
Let me be green
sea turtles, giant leatherbacks
and loggerheads new born,
that circumvent the continents undaunted
only to return twenty years later
to lay their eggs on the very beach
where they themselves hatched
following beckoning fingers
of moonlight
back into the cold dark sea.

Can they taste footprints
borne on waves from a distant shore?
Might they hear the Earth
sing its silent magnetic song?
Do the imprint of stars whisper
in their brains the way to go home?
How do they know?

I replay the melody of a song
some twenty years deep
buried in my life
and the lyrics come back
in waves, like a map.
I sing, pulling up the nets
of memory; faces, places
and odd small events, even scents
find their way to the surface,
haunting familiar faces
I once wore, a watery trail
that leads
to who I have become.

The pearl moonlight whispers,
"It is time,
   time to remember…"

The Great Divide
(Notes From A Reading)

Wearing only sunlight
a faceless woman sits poised
before an existential window.

What blended, raw elements
of color constitute
her mystic luminescence;
rust, ash, dried blood,
smoke mixed with semen,
the oxidation of bronze?

Like hypnotic regression,
paintings on the walls
mix memories with dreams;
the breasts that nursed
and comforted me, Paris streets
where I wrote poetry
on the sidewalks with chalk
dipped in Chardonnay,
a pair of empty boots
at ease with themselves
exuding such singular identity
I'm sure I've worn them
content now without me
and the young guitarist
that sooths without a sound.

From her unseen chair
the woman rises, older now,
crossing the great divide
between perception and reality,
of cultures, continents, decades,
wars and atrocities
to kneel
before a coffee table
cutting a sliver of pungent cheese,
the slow knife whispering
reflections of the child
trapped within.

Is this the hard
ripened milk of memories
that nursed our fragmented childhoods?
"Look at me Daddy! Look at me!"
she cries back to the vacant canvas.

In the implied window
his mute reflection stands
unmovable, steadfast
in his stubborn resolve
like an iron horse in the rain.

Johnny Picasso's
(A Coffee Shop in Anacortes, WA)

The photographs
that decorate the wall
in the corner of the coffee shop
are windows to wishes
that cover the holes
in someone's life
and the fan on the ceiling
turns and turns
rustling the pages of time.

The old couple
seated by the window
holding hands
are back on their first date.
The pierced teenager
at the counter
waiting for his cappuccino
is a now man,
casting his own bitter regrets,
while the fan on the ceiling
turns and turns
stirring the brief silence
when the cafe is again empty,
the muted restraining
between a gasp and a scream
like the faint dust
suspended
in a momentary silhouette
of sunlight;
a life unchallenged.

Sweet Bliss

Hidden mystery lies
in the grain of wood
like the dark
swirling surface
of a distant planet
a hint
the intoxicating
possibility
of a smile
that could change everything
in the way blooming jasmine
makes tangible the elusive
still night air
for no other reason
than that I should breathe
deeply in, not how a candle
extinguishes itself
but when every burning question
is contently withdrawn.

The Lake

A once secluded lake, surrounded
by Australian pine and cypress woods
was my boyhood retreat.
The grandest of those lofty pines,
supple like a whip, supported a rope swing
that cooled many a Florida summer,
stood like a guard over late night campfires
where the metal of friendships were forged.

Gone now are the rugged limestone banks,
layers of pine needles that carpeted the shoreline.
The leveled perimeter is now mowed grass.
Cookie-cutter houses, shoulder to shoulder,
line the shore, with an elaborate fountain
in the middle of the lake
like a mammoth crystal lily.

A lone anhinga perches off shore
on the barely visible branch
of a submerged tree, as if there existed
a lost forest beneath the surface of the water
and he stood where two worlds meet,
standing on the water, motionless
with wet wings raised
against the setting sun
as though some ancient god
frozen in timeless worship.

Now, no sense of adventure stirs here,
nor rite of passage soars, far out
over forbearing waters deathless and free.
No dreams or schemes dance bright
like hot sparks offered up
to a night sky full of stars.

The tall wind that once screamed
through wispy pines
is silent now.
Does it know me still,
or have I too
become concrete?

Silent Reaches
(or The Healing Power Of Jazz)

Outside my window
and across the way
the trees wait,
having dismissed the beggar wind.
They wait with their long
still beards of Spanish moss,
squirrel infested,
wait like loyal scribes
for me to conceive
and come forth
with some deathless wisdom.
I have none.
I offer only blank paper.
I lay myself open and bare.
Write on me O cypress sages
with your blinding arrows
of platinum glimmer!
Through leafed depths whisper
to me ancient secrets
in hollow tongues
like angry water
brought down
through lightning's thunder
to hidden springs broken.
Suck me
into your roots.
Searching day and life
at my window
I know only that free men
see a barred world,
that only those
who have been behind bars
see the world as truly free.

I know there is a loneliness
that can orchestrate the tidal noise
of traffic, the incoherence
of crowded voices
into a silence deeper than death,
that there are tender spaces
between the tears of a friend
that only a touch can comprehend,
that the hushed silence of love
largely, is a selfish hunger
feeding upon itself
and there exists wordless depths,
silent reaches
within my search for meaning,
within the pain and craving of desire
that can only be reached, touched
by the unchained cry
of a raging saxophone.

Cafe Gypsies

He assures her stars
are not frightened of the day.
Only in the hollow darkness
of their own souls
do men become aware
of distant light he tells her, using words
the way Michelangelo used a chisel.
They crossed paths, met like an idea
entering a mind, from which he carries
in his heart her dreams, as if
they were an unborn child.
He lives the way he eats, hungrily
tearing truth from the bone
of experience. Slobbering street wisdom
like a construction worker,
he erects in our hearts
towers of vision,
while she sips cappuccino
like Nefertiti in cowboy boots.
Although, he cannot see the pyramids
of doubt and deception
in her black eyes.
We leave the cafe all holding hands,
something about a world going on outside
and homeless mankind
on a cosmic street corner bench
called Earth, selfishly clutching
his scavenger belongings, clothed
yet naked, all fighting for the best seat.
All the while missing the bus
and how we must not miss it, "STOP!
LOOK..." (He always makes us look
at things we do not want to see,
or where before we saw nothing.) "Shhh.."
he tells us, all still holding hands.

Then cloud cover parts
over an empty field across the street.
Suddenly downy tops of broom sedge
light up like matches
struck against the sunset, thin
ragged vagabonds with psychic auras.
"Each one is blind," he whispers,
"yet they know every star by name."

A Poet Once Lived Here

It sits upon a hill.
There are no floors.
The whole house
is knee-deep
in wild flowers.
You can feel the cool
moist earth
between your toes
as you move
from room to room.

In the house
there are many windows,
windows that look out
over oceans, mountains,
across the stars, down subways,
into the gutters and alleys
where broken winos lay
and where no windows are
there are no walls
only mirrors
with bludgeoned
bloodied cracks.

Two towers rise
out of the serenity
of the backyard
like lighthouses;
imagery and truth.
I have stood
upon those towers
and pondered
piercing landscapes,
yet I fear now
the doors
are forever
locked.

Ghosts Harvest

Rich farmland
that brought forth a mountain
of blood red tomatoes
and transcendent strawberries
over decades past
has become a strip mall.

The seasons of my life
ebbed and flourished
around the quiet consistency
of its agrarian cycles.
Over the years
against its rooted relevance
I measured the fruits
of my life,
equally justifying
dry times
of fruitless growth.

At times I felt
as a lost wayfarer
having somehow
wandered in
off the far fields.
Its fertile expanse
was a visible touchstone
an oasis
amid the concrete
confusion.

Now, driving past
in the uncertain
half-light of daybreak,
I see the young staked plants
in endless rows
spanning the empty
parking lot
and in the dizzy heat
of mid day, reflected
in the store front windows
I glimpse the migrant workers,
faceless under straw hats,
bent and scattered
digging among the rows
like ticks on a dog.

Mute among them
I spot a vestige of myself
scratching for roots,
gleaning shards
of significance.

Well Of Shadows

Memory is a dead crooked stick
with which we prod the darkness,
banishing ghosts from under the bed.

Beginning on flat land laced with bog,
once the bed of an ancient lake,
I hike with my walking stick
up Boone Fork Trail,
past bloodroot and mountain laurel,
under the shade of maples
and white bark birch
that propagate the alluring
whispers of a nearby waterfall.
There will be huge granite rocks
to climb, daring jumps to execute.
I ascend reverently through canopies
of rhododendron still in bloom
as though on holy ground,
their pale blossoms
strewn across the path.

At 52 years old I walk alone
tethered to a team of ghosts
held in stride, dependent
upon one another's footing.
Ahead of me, I at 40 climb, then
of 30, on to where, at the lead,
a 10 year old me marches,
cradling myself newborn.
Behind me, slowing the pace,
denominations of myself extend back
through the next-to-the last, who helps
steady along my final faltering self,
Moses ascending mount Nebo
to overlook the promised land of Canaan.

With age, my life has come
to resemble a deep well.
I fear what lies forgotten
beneath its darkness.

By Fire

On the eastern shoreline,
at the rocky edge of Lake Jackson,
I stoop to dip my fingers
in the cool still water
as if to touch the heart, the essence
of the Grand Teton mountains
that rise massive
along the western shore.
Before language, deeper
than understanding,
my spirit touches theirs.
The sage wind at my back
is curious, prodding, running
excited through the close trees.
Only the Quaking Aspen are talking.

I make my way back up,
onto the Swan Lake
and Heron Pond Loop
with an eye open
for a good walking stick.
Each trail provides its own
whose native wood
instinctively knows every fork
and hidden bend encountered.

Blue Wasatch and Red Firecracker
Snapdragons surround the trail
like silent angelic spectators.
In a millisecond, the delicate
downy seed globes of dandelions
capture and release
the late afternoon sunlight,
as if to give it new meaning.
I bend down, and with one
breath and a wish, scatter its tiny
parachute bristles to the wind.

As I walk further on,
the waxy serotinous cones
of the Lodgepole pine crunch
under my inattentive steps.
Have I become like them?
Does it take the intense heat,
the lightening strike fires
of adverse circumstance
to release my potential,
that which I have to offer,
to pass on to others?

Evening begins to settle in
over Swan Lake.
I head back to Colter Bay.
Elk seeking drink
and beaver quietly swimming
among the yellow pond lilies
gift their presence.
A steady cool
twilight breeze begins to blow
and down through the ethereal
amber glow, the Cottonwood
blossoms fall
faint like snow.

With this journey nearing
its end, I must depart
somewhat disappointed
at having not witnessed
the rare Trumpeter Swan.
Yet, I am content,
for the passion of my quest,
the desire of my dream
is still intact.

El Lector

His voice was light
eroding through futility,
imparting to its listeners
identity, the way smoke
from a fine cigar
slowly exhaled
defines the surrounding air.

The stories he read
moistened
and held together
limp hearts
long dried out
by the hot
mundane factories
like the tobacco leaves
they stripped, day after day,
sweating out their despair.

Their hands flow
through independent
repetitions
as the lector reads
rolling each cigar
like gentle waves
repeatedly grabbing
the shores of Havana
and folding the sand.

The passion and the intrigue
his stories bring
filter down
through their fingers
as silently
they roll up their dreams

flavoring each cigar
with the mystery
of their lives.

Unopened
(for Mark)

There is a farm in the hills,
back in the far country
of boyhood, where shadows
of the hickory trees run long
and deep. The familiar
roads are not open there.
In the house
where it was hard to grow
lives an angry old bear
that growls at anyone
who goes near, even frightens
the grandchildren away.

The rocks on the road
leading up to the house,
that I have not seen for so long,
are sharp and cruel. Still,
we removed our shoes,
my brother and I, and trudged
up that endless quarter mile
to Golgotha,
to no avail.

Now that old bear
lies dead in the house,
all the meanness
embalmed out of him,
(I touch his fur)
less frightening now,
frail, from years of holding on
to poisonous pride
and unforgiving anger
that made him seem
fearless, hid the fact

that he lacked the courage
to ever let down his guard
long enough to learn how to love,
as if letters of reconciliation
too painful to open, written with a pen
driven through the palm of a hand,
tossed in the back of some drawer
for maybe, maybe tomorrow,
a drawer that death forever locked.

Alcatraz

It sits like Earth itself, a harsh rock
in the midst of a cold sea of separation,
where men die from the inside out,
crushed beneath cement-heavy hopelessness,
caged in the iron-rusty despair of their own actions.
Only their dreams escape
into a darkness barred by distant lights
and become seagulls returning with the morning
to crap all over the walls and fences,
their excrement slowly eroding the structures.

Constricting cells hold a deadened emptiness
that lingers, even now, with the finality of judgment.
Pale walls are piercing opaque mirrors that silently
and relentlessly taunt. The stale air is made up
of the last breaths of desperate dying men,
their mute ghosts locked in the shadows,
lost in the echoes. There are prisons
within me of fear, addiction and failure,
where I am both jailor and inmate.

On the hill overlooking the bay,
all that remains of the warden's house
are bare unfinished cinder walls, no doors,
no floors, no roof, only a few center beams.
Wild flowers fill the house waist-high dancing
around the fireplace in the living room, Nasturtium,
Valerian, Bear's Breech and Honeysuckle,
sprinkled with Red Hot Poker. Seagulls perch
on the remaining rafters over what was once
the dining area. One sits in an empty frameless window.
All as if to say, there are hard scars that remain,
yet the demons are gone, beauty and healing
have prevailed, life is bursting forth unchained!

Yet, deep, crouched in the solitary stillness,
the confining hack-sawed darkness, barred
by the cracked light of an open cell door,
there, scratched in the far corner
on a wall, I saw my initials.

In The Course Of Constellations

There is a black hole forming
on the back of Ursa Major's paw.
It signals the demise
of dazzling brilliance, vibrant
starlight sucked into cold oblivion.
For centuries the virile bear
roamed invincible, unchanged.
Now do the flood locks
of merciless time
begin to let loose.

I walk mountain trails
in the moonlight far below,
across streams of ancient water
evaporated, precipitated, filtered
over and over again. Atoms
of Centurions and Union soldiers,
kings and settlers are assimilated
into leaves of sourwood, ash, beech,
and sugarberry. An unexpected wind
whips their branches, do they remember
war, or dance in silent unison.

It took you a week
to hear the stillness in the woods
that gave you short stories of your life,
the quiet to which you will return.
Down many trails, together
we've found our way, so many paths
have led to our discovery, and yet,
so much has been forgotten,
taken for granted
that I must pretend
we've only met
for the first time.

Roads Of Remembrance

I am drowning
in a flood of memories.
There are pieces of me
down every street, children
of various ages running in terror
as from a time bomb, covered
in the napalm of nostalgia.
Burned in fragments
of summer, scents
of flowers
I knew only as a child
haunt me.

At the head of the street
I grew up on, though once
a neighborhood thruway,
stands a Dead End sign.
Perhaps symbolic
of seeking the past.

Construction crews reconfigure
once familiar landscape
that seems now, alien terrain.

Bristling blossom stalks
cover the dense mango trees
like antenna, further away,
like new fallen snow,
as though they were
trying to become
something
other
than what they were.

There are quiet streets
I fear to go down,
the memories so thick,
hidden so deep,
I might never return.

Wooden Crosses

There are holes in the garden wall,
escape routes through the briar hedge
of time and space, marked
with make-shift wooden crosses.
Where do the cherished ones go
when all the king's horses
and all the king's men
can't put them back
together again; head-on
into the certainty of God.

A somber sun sets
on busy intersections and
lonely stretches of interstate
wearing the twilight-
plaided asphalt
like a Glengarry,
while the bagpipe wind moans
as it gleans the dying oak leaves
from reluctant trees,
wrapping burning arms
of gold and seared orange
around rocky shoulders
and broken guard rails
like a desperate lover
lost in soul-searching's
imparted silence, reaching
for reasons that justify.

Assumption is a drunk, silent killer.

Go push your platitudes,
say time heals
to the young widow
dancing, eyes closed,
in the cold
quivering rain
with one arm
around a ghost.

Leaves

All the stars have fallen,
barely glistening now,
among the fresh cut grass
of my back yard.
The white birds of morning
have landed
and begun their foraging.

Leftover mist from the cool
of night, gathered together
in hidden pockets like guilt
finds no place in warm sunlight
that holds aloft a pale prisoner moon
stolen from the darkness.

I decide, after coffee, to rake
together the dead oak leaves
that the playful March wind
swirls in circles like regret
in front of the garage, undecided
if I, myself, am still clinging
to the green stem, or in release
to the downward discoloring winds.

The shifting leaves
sweep across my path,
clicking like turning pages
in the great lexicon of change.
I rake and rake as if
trying to uncover innocence.
A sense of urgency fills the void
where we lack closure, unable
to recognize completeness
in a cyclic, transitional world.

The purpose is to get all the leaves
into orderly piles to be bagged
and discarded I explain, though my
young sons view the beckoning heaps
as giant pillows to be dove upon.

I rake together
the last remaining leaves
as new ones break free
and begin their descent.

Perfect Day

You decide God
is air
as you swing
strong
impervious
to scrapes and falls
through sunshine
so pure and perfect
the very leaves
on the trees
seem holy
all clouds
are banished
and you ask me
where heaven is.

Lost In Flight

Swaying trees dream
in the flowing locks
of a little girl's hair
as she runs with the summer
breeze chasing black birds
that caw and glisten purple
in the doubtless blinding sun
and the wind wishes
in the glee of her laughter
that it too could caw back
and the fleeing shimmering
black birds retreat
to the safety of tall oaks
while little Lenore reborn
with arms stretched out
like wings
weaves and circles below
through the sunlight
and the summer
circles, circles ever more.

Westview Cemetery

A sparse, unkempt cemetery
scarcely more
than a pitiful sand lot
too impoverished for head stones
hides behind ficus hedges
along Copans Road.
Cement sarcophagus lids lie
among the short cropped weeds
like litter from passing cars
gathered by the wind.

The weathered cemetery sits
next to the old Pilot Steel works
as if to be close to life,
as though its shadow, hard
and unforgiving as iron
with bent dreams that rust in the sun
and the cars go by, day and night,
night and day, unaware
of a starkness so sad
as to not even be frightening,
yet it haunts me, follows me
in the car, across town, up
the driveway and into my bed
in the weighing stillness of night.

I have never walked there, yet
I would recognize it in the darkness
of dreams that let slip- that you can
actually fly, thirty or so feet
above the trees, dipping
like a roller coaster
to touch with your toes
their tickly tops
and the hard dark ground

rushing to your cheek with a thud
and you live, laughing
as the moon looms low in the distant
trees like a gentle traveler.

Perhaps, it is all the dreams
that were too big
to come true, all rolled together
to illuminate the darkness
and inspire lovers
and the cars go by
night and day, day and night,
unaware. At first,
I thought it horribly wrong,
a dishonor to the dead,
to languish in such poverty.

But perhaps we perpetrate a lie
in keeping graveyards so
adorned and well manicured
as though death were neat
and rich, keeper of the spoils,
steeling all that we struggle
so desperately to hold on to.

Ah, but love's faith gleams,
winks from the hot sand
among the weeds in Westview,
exposing Death for the liar he is.
Like the rusty latch on the gate
into the old cemetery,
he merely unlocks
the prison doors.

The Painting

It hung in the living room
above the sofa, in the house
where I was a child.

The large oil canvas portrayed a path
through shaded woods that rose
over a lightsome hill
between two large Australian pines.
Viewed only from behind,
a dark mysterious
cloaked figure of a man
with a walking stick
ascended the path, poised
to disappear beyond the hill.

The wild brush of imagination
would paint myriad dreams
on the eyes of my youthful heart
as I would stare with intrigue
at the grandfather figure.
I wanted to follow, run
to take his hand, tag along
over that wondrous, enchanted hill.

The woods were peaceful,
the colors soft and subtle.
No drunken rages echoed
in that dim, still air.
The other side of that hill was mine!
I painted the landscape, drafted
the scenery and completed the story.
And yet, somehow, I never really did.

If you stare at a light long enough,
then close your eyes,
the image remains.

The youthful chapter of my life
closed with the doors
of that old house,
yet the image of the painting
remained, forever in my mind's eye.

Though, perhaps the man was not
quite so old, just simply a father
on his way home.

The old path still beckoned me,
beyond the hill still drew me.
Though maybe,
it was quite simply
just another hill,
just another path
that lay beyond the other side.
Yet it remained a safe place,
a quiet spot.

As the years drew on,
the woods seemed darker,
beyond the hill lighter,
perhaps a sunrise,
or is it a sunset?
I can no longer tell.
It scares me, that
ominous hill. I hesitate
to cross it.

And yet, now, the thing
that frightens me most,
I know that man...

The Hands Of Time

Where does time go
once it is used, played
with the whisper
of a turned page,
dissolved in the smoke
of a burnt candle?
Like endless waves
that beach themselves
thinning to the tiniest tip
of a millisecond,
each(the same)now
retreats, disassembles, reforms
only to wash ashore
again and again.

The question then becomes
not where does time go
but who do we become
once the moment washes over us?
For we are the visible
hands of time
that glide through the stilled
air of hope
like a held breath,
a hushed promise,
lopping of chunks of now
that crumble into memories
and regrets, which tumble
down the corridor
of then
like the echo
of a heart's final
(tic..) desperate
beat (..toc).

The Fountain

Vaporized, high altitude
water molecules
become letters of hope
hammered by freezing air
into snowflakes, each
characters in a crystal alphabet
more intricate than Chinese
spoken only between God and angels,
autonomous truths slipped from Heaven,
delivered by the wind,
then posted on the gaunt
stark windows of a lobby
in an office building
illuminated by the distant sun,
while the wind whispers, "Look,
they hold the answers to every prayer…"
as the large open air lobby
bustles with quiet, hectic indifference
driven by cold numbers.

In the center of the lobby
around the elevators
winds an elaborate fountain
and the snowflakes
put their hands on the windows
and press their tiny faces
against the glass like children
watching everyone
walk by in their sleep
around the fountain with its curves
that live beyond abrupt corners like hope
feeding bushes of surprise
and glittering seeds of dreams
light on the bare surface
of the water

in the fountain
without a single coin
where no one
makes a wish,
while outside
the snowflakes
turn to tears,
to one day
join the fountain.

Listen

I have worked so long and so hard
against circumstance and uncertainty
the hammer and anvil
that beat our minds into swords,
hearts into plowshares
and our poor damned souls
never knowing
which one to trust.
I have worked so long and so hard
baking bricks, or is it bread
I can no longer tell
the difference anymore,
the oven's fires raging deep
into my soul
where fierce pomes are formed
like blown glass
delicate as truth
to throw at death and run.
I have worked so long and so hard
that I have forgotten what it was
that I was working for
until tonight,
when I saw the faces
of my sleeping children.
Then again, if I wasn't so tired
lying out here in the grass
in the back yard at 11:00 P.M.
under the soothing stars
of a clear January night
might seem a little crazy
and I wouldn't hear God
use cricket legs
to sing His poems to me,
the ones He worked on
so long and so hard.

My Father's Grave

The delirious reds of feverish dusk
spread across the burning sky
like a terminal disease.
At that moment, when the sun
breathes its last golden breath
then slips, just beyond the horizon
leaving the entire world
bathed in the eerie amber glow
of Heaven's porch light,
I laid down on the grass
above my father's grave
and stretched myself rigid,
assuming the position
I guessed to be his.

Why did I come?
What was I seeking,
a ghost, a memory,
a child's myth, or a man
such as myself?
Beds of grass
cradle not our loved ones,
far gone from this world.
We visit but earthen shrines
of dust, upon which we offer
the sacrifice of tears
for the redemption of our regrets.
I cried for the battles
he fought and lost.
I cried for the demons
from which he could not free himself.
I cried for the grandchildren
he will never know.
I felt his spiraling thirst swallow me,

the numbing alcohol that drained
life and dignity from him.
I sunk deep into his prejudices,
felt them poison what was left
of my heart, make it hard
as dry bones.

I considered then, his roots.
I remembered too, his gentleness,
his humor, his support
and encouragement,
the many skills he taught me.
I felt my heart breathe again
and again, tears found my eyes.

Part of me lies buried with him,
the child I was, while part of him
lives on in me.
He was my age now, when I,
as a young boy laughed and played
in this same cemetery, unaware
of its depth, that eternity stood
in the shadows of these timeless trees.
Though in different times
and in our individual ways,
we each pass through the same
stages of life, become the same ages,
yet never equal, always the father,
always the son.
I wept because I still needed a father,
and I wept because I no longer did.

I opened my eyes in the darkness,
rose and brushed the grass
from my clothes.
Walking away from the grave
my steps were light

and aware like a ghost,
hallowed and humble
as a pilgrim. I know now
who I am, why I am.
Death cleanses love,
while love bridges death.

For A Moment

The smell of life
your hair full of sun
we fill your little pool
with dreams
a spider in the grass
bees and a butterfly
on the pentas
set us off
on an exploration
creating
and reforming the world
with delicious mud
painting our chests
for the ritual dance
across the air
we make rainbows
with the garden hose
while time hold's its breath
for this
is Heaven.

Lost Oceans

You share with me
your weighty decisions,
staying the pendulum
between friendship and love,
hearts hung in the balance.
For this I love you
and feel like a father again.

I offer wisdom
gleaned of my own
experience, yet
wisdom cannot be given,
it must be purchased
with the pain
of your own error.
I could tell you
of my own mistakes,
but they too
are minted in the coinage
of another time and place,
rare in value to me,
yet not valid tender
for your debts.
You must mint your own.

You ask me
what I wanted to be
when I was your age
and lost treasures wash ashore.
I reflect over shells
of forgotten dreams.
The animal that once
inhabited them
has long since gone,
moved on to a bigger shell,

more rock-like, lots of room
to fancy, yet highly immobile.
The finer, more intricate
shells of youth, bold
in delicate design so fragile,
borne on secret currents
from adventurous islands,
lay empty now, but for the echo
of waves of regret
breaking along distant
shores of compromise.
If you hold one to your heart,
you can hear a lost ocean cry.

Silent Touch

Exploring the woods
with my young son,
I lecture on life's cycle,
fallen trees half buried
in pine needles,
slowly returning to the soil.

Hiking, we come upon
a dead Australian pine
standing naked,
all dry and hard,
its smooth bare trunk
engraved with squiggly scars
like some ancient cave markings
where worms had tunneled
beneath the bark.

While I ran
my fingers upward
over the ghostly
hieroglyphics
as if it were Braille
holding some omnipotent
message from beyond
the grave, sunlight broke
through the tree tops
like an omen, blinding me.
Did I really
want to unlock
that door?

I held my breath–
one of the markings
matched the lines
in the palm
of my hand.

The Sandbox

I begin as an unwitting partner,
a mere spectator to my son,
after all, it's just sand. Although,
it does feel good to bury your feet,
to let the fine white grains
flow cool off a spade, free
as a thousand pointless cares,
pour from a pail like memories,
the hour glass of the timeless.

Sand holds the secrets of the earth
inked in elements,
inscribed in the hieroglyphics
of molecules, deciphered only
when we move slow as field grass.
Sand contains the chaff of stars,
ancient kingdoms ground to dust,
the matrix key that unlocks spring.
Perhaps sand is the great river of time itself,
from which all things emerge,
upon which they ride,
and unto which they return.

Inherently dry, sand lacks cohesiveness
in and of itself. If disturbed,
it caves in quicker than confidence,
only to cease as sudden as life.
We try to construct out of it permanence,
only to find that it holds only hints
of our intentions. The only binding
source of moisture
is from eyes of pain and sorrow.

Tunneling, we uncover dinosaurs
that we had forgotten were buried.
Unlike the grave, sand lets us hide nothing.
With toy cups we scoop and dump,
piling sand from one spot to another
with reason and purpose unknown
perhaps even to my son.
The sand becomes many things.

As you fill, then slowly empty your cup,
what is it that you see flowing out?
Is it wealth, is it power, is it sensual?
It's all so silly I remind myself,
sitting in this plastic box,
after all, it's just sand.

The Wait

Will it be
in the quiet of night
that Grandma leaves,
in the dark
when the world
seems to hold its breath
and hope
can be as easily abandoned
as embraced?

Or will it be
in the calm
clear morning
when night's restless
dreams seem foolish
as dawn comes silent
and all encompassing
like a resurrection?

Will it happen
in the rain
when thunder
sounds like God
calling her name
and lightening
reaches down
like a bridge?

When at last
the grueling wait
succumbs to quiet fate,
I shall weep in the shadows
of loss and need,
then rise and set a course
far clear from the reefs

of regret,
light a candle
in my heart
and cherish
her entering in
to the perfect city
of endless light.

Echoes In The Wind

There is a certain angle
when you swing on a swing,
if you tilt your head back
just right,
to where the sun shines
right in your eyes
and you close them
and become a child again
and the wind,
the wind remembers,
brushing your hair
across your face
like a magic wand,
brushing back the years.

Back in the distance,
in the hushed rush of the wind,
you hear the contentment
of your mother's heart,
there in the wind-hung silence
the moment
before she calls
you home.

Discovery

Stars in the lost and lonely
night, sharp beacons
from somewhere far
and long ago
teach old sea captains
the way home.
My old poems are teachers.
Beneath their waves
of inspiration
I become coral, colorful
and wondrously varied,
porous from the pain
of growing,
yet stationary,
letting the cold tides
of criticism flow silently
through me, over me,
hoping to glean food
beyond the last line
silence leads me
down to the hidden
spring that runs
beneath all words
and I relearn
who it is
that I am.

The Flight Of The Poet

I have held the hand of sickness
through a night in Hell
until the sharp light of morning
slit our eyelids like a scalpel.
I have looked down
condemned men's eyes
deep enough to see
we are all on Death Row.
I will drink full
the measure of my cup.
I will rise above searing fields
steeped in cool mist, blind
with first sun in my eyes, seeing
back beyond words, singing
flaming spasms of creation surging
from the encoded matrix of my soul
down through time
to the moment
of timelessness,
like a ragged moth
to some cosmic porch light.

Baby's Room

I finished painting
your room today,
both excited and nervous,
wondering, if tonight
you might be born.

I only wish I could
paint your world
with gentler colors,
paper over
the ugly spots,
but then it wouldn't
be your world,
or even mine.

The hard colors
will make you reach
for gentleness within.
The ugly spots
will give you faith
to free the dreams
that beat within the cages
of your heart.

It is not then perfection
which defines beauty,
but rather, the courage
of the wounded.

Song Of Refuge

I defend my love,
divide my time
between parents.

There is a place
where we meet,
behind sentimental
walls of melody,
beneath a roof
of familiar harmony.
Gutted silence
its only furniture,
this room of a song
holds but two chairs,
their backs
to each other.
Mine is the mute
face in a picture
in a corner behind
cracked glass.

Memorized lyrics
no longer holding
meaning,
they each
separately
hum
with their
eyes closed,
not noticing,
not remembering
how unspoken words
shatter glass.

The Long Walk Home

I couldn't have been
more than three
years old when,
late in the evening,
my father took me
for a walk after dinner.
It was a long
adventurous journey.
Gradually
the neighborhood grew
frighteningly unfamiliar
and I,
weary and unable
to go on any further.

My father scooping me up
in his strong invisible arms,
holding my nodding head,
resting it against his shoulder
as he carried me
on into the darkness
was the last thing
I remembered.

When I awoke
and opened my eyes
in the bird hushed
beauty of morning,
the bed-snug warmth
of home,
the first thing
that I saw
was him smiling
big as life.
He bent down,
kissed me and whispered,
"This is what dying is like."

Across The Anvil

What formative rivers
have gouged tenderness
and punched
understanding
into gentle men's
eyes; dark stones
made smooth
under pounding
white water
clear as vodka?
How did they
translate
stifled fears
of back-handed
silence to tender
their quiet gaze
into such
potent medicine?
Condemned love
forged firm,
battered flat
across an anvil
of abusive years,
etching eyes
that would haunt
an executioner.

When the icy
gray waters of time
smooth the innocence
from my eyes,
erode and redefine
the shores of my face,
will they be as kind?

Images

An impressionistically grainy
black and white photograph
depicts my grandmother
and grandfather
in a field full of summer.
They are carefree and young,
though their dated clothes
and period hair styles
make them seem older.

Their love for each other
is as apparent as the breeze
that stirs my grandmother's
long white dress. With one hand,
she attempts to hold it
modestly in place
at her knees, keeping her hair
from her face with the other
hand. She is smiling
as my grandfather hugs her
from the side.

Yet, all this vivid motion
of life and unfolding
destiny is frozen
as the rustling dress.
Its movement is implied,
much like time itself,
like mute moonlight
on new, tender leaves
in a death-still night.

We remain locked
in change, yet frozen
in the ever present, all
progressive development
is implied.
To the past; we are
the invisible light
that etches images,
to the future;
a voiceless still life.

Life Cycle

So then God scattered
pieces of the puzzle
all across time
which became everyone's
eyes, how we look
to one another
trying to piece together
our hearts
are corked messages
(there is a poet dying inside me)
stopped in the bottle
of our fears, adrift
on the sea of chance
childhood dreams
are bright kites
caught in the twisted
aging trees
of circumstance
power lines
telephone lines
last lines
of poems
upon which your
mind perches
then takes to flight
as a poet is born
inside you.

Ghost Crossing

I followed
a wooded path
that dipped down
crossing an old
dry river bed
which once held life
and now life
of a different sort.

Arched trees
lining what were
once banks
whisper in sunlight
tales of fish rippling
over the strewn
pine needles.
Sun-pierced shadows
dream reflections;
long forgotten
faces of Indians.
Wild flowers
dance in tribute
to the life
the river
once supported.

Within my life
are river beds
of change
where I fear
to cross
and pause
groping
for the phantom
currents
of stagnation.

Free Fall

The stilled rage
of burnt wood
odor
cured sweet
with rain
still lingers long
after the fire
doubt sets in
suffocating clinging
shy little girl
she sees within
my bourbon-depraved
bitterness
my next poem
us falling
between the lines
always bigger
than a hope
smaller than a promise
even broken
her love's believing
makes rhyme of uncertainty
and pens the bravery
of my darkness.

The Measure Of Distance

Destiny
from time to time
languishes the way
an old poet sits,
stoic with his drink
and his dated music,
feeling in a language
beyond words
while his life
haunts him
like a train
singing across the night,
crying between the rails,
between what was
and what might have been,
faint from a distance,
steady and soothing
like hope, up close
frighteningly deafening
like the heart thunder
of desperation.

Where Lost Rivers Run

On the outskirts of childhood,
at the edge of memory,
a worn two lane road stretches
into the future, bordered
along the edge by a river
like an important word
heavily underlined.

Though scarcely more than a ditch,
it became a sanctuary
for the restless heart of youth,
a place of focus
where pressured aspirations
paused to breathe, a garden refuge
of divine communion like Eden,
buried now and forever lost.
Now the Cherubim's
flaming swords of change
bar forever the visible gate,
nevermore to be seen.
Are you there, running still
beneath the black asphalt
as silently as dreams in the night,
covered in raging blossoms,
hyacinth's pink and purple blooms?

It was there, on the rocky banks,
that I first glanced
into the water's murky face
and discovered a poet looking back.
All filled in and covered up now
is the river, the road paved over,
six lanes wide, smooth and hypnotic.
Before, the patched and pot-holed
bumpy road dipped and bounced

like a horseback ride. Shoulderless
and narrow, the road and river
ran as one, while danger
rode the edge like adolescence,
tarred wooden telephone poles
shooting past drag racing teenagers
like stick men
falling down an elevator shaft.

There is little danger now to life,
no excitement of risk taken,
only the sad tragedy
of falling asleep at the wheel.

Part of me sleeps,
buried with that river
beneath the hard asphalt,
buried like a dormant seed,
like robbed childhood
layers beneath a rocky foundation.

At one time farmland fed by the river,
green and sunny, spread out
from either side of the road
to the ends of the horizon,
fresh, impressionable earth
eager to be plowed and furrowed,
to bring forth substance.

Now the used land lays barren,
stripped of dreams and convictions,
leveled and cleared like a bought woman
ready for the consummation
of commercialization.
What kind of buildings will rise now,
positive, thriving structures,
or cold cement monuments to compulsion?

How many more lost rivers,
like severed roots, run silent
beneath our busy highways, paved over
like awkward first impressions?

On the outskirts of childhood,
at the edge of memory,
I moisten my scarred roots
with the eye-mist of nostalgia,
for once a river ran
with raging blossoms,
now there lies a road,
and I walk on water.

Fallen Blossoms

Tabebuia trees
grasp the air full bloom,
like flaming hands
of yellow fire. Each
a prom princess, all
in summer bright, timeless
captured innocence, budding,
softly spoken desire.

Bent from trusting the wind,
they lean into the sun
like hungry love,
their rough, thick bark
soft to the touch,
breakable as friendship.
Pressed, they cast off
weakened leaves
to the uncommitting wind.

Are they setting free
impossible dreams
of an endless summer
forever green, or letting go
of their children,
tossing the desperate dice
of last chances,
of tomorrows
that others own?

Fallen blossoms
litter the unmowed grass
like fading yellow suns
in a galaxy of green,
lay dying in the dirt
like a thousand
jilted dreams
of love,
like virginity.

Eternity

And so time died
of old age
unthen and whenless
or perhaps boredom
all the souls
of those who became
characters
in her
stories
and believed them, all
holding her
hand like obedient
grandchildren
too innocent
to be frightened
the colored balloons
of now
have all
popped themselves
in the tall cool grass
of oblivion
let us lie on our backs
and imagine faces
in the circular clouds
of forever
whispering tales
of bravery
silently feeling
the dying
of another birth.

Trophies Of Ego

Beauty dependent
solely upon itself
is made prey.

There are those,
soulless hunters,
who would shoot
arrows of lies
through the heart
of her dreams
of love,
spill the clear
fertile blood
of her trust
in the barren valleys
of comfortless comforters,
discarding her tender carcass
to the dogs of memory.

Severing heads from minds,
skinning souls of body,
they seek to mount her breasts
on the stone walls of their ego
like charging horns
fierce with passion
short lived,
hunting in vain
for love.

Echoes Of Destiny

Focus
begins in the heart,
not in the mind's eye.
Lost, ritual becomes
routine, while routines
become rituals.

There are temptations
too strong,
cages
that bear my name.

The unanchored heart
is a blind slave
content
in the chains
of its own choosing.
For the battlefields
of destiny
are strewn
not with broken swords
of will,
but with shrill echoes
of regret
over the choice
of allegiance.

The Gift Of Words

An art medium
both deaf and blind,
theirs is not
a crystalline world
of rapturous song,
nor dramatic display
of theatrical flair,
no legacy of carved marble,
nor weighty statements
cast in bronze,
not a canvas symphony
of color and depth,
textured crescendo
of tones and shapes,
only the flat dimension
of black printed type,
Braille for the heart.
Rather,
poets are sad,
sympathetic clowns
on the street corners
of life,
who blow up
long balloons
of ideas,
twisting and tying them
in knots of feeling,
creating for us
strange and wonderful
creatures
to take home.

The Braille Brief, And Beyond

Sparrows at random
sit along power line
staffs like a score of music
most (probably) likely
definitely maybe
absolutely
perhaps
jazz
while a sea gull becomes the wind-
white winter abreast wings
of gray misty dawn
edged with starless night
over valleys stilled with autumn.

An occasional stone's mossy head
peeks through the fallen leaves
the fierce naked trees
on hilltop
with their crooked fingers
claw the misty horizon
until its gray unblinking eyes bleed sunset
tell of wind- quiet wind, secret wind
as it plays the pine
like a careful instrument
of entrancing fragility
mood- deep, distant
can I grasp it?
or merely an obscure feeling I once had,
a poem that went unwritten.

I think the mirror-still stream
is really a long
magical window (am I
on the outside looking in-
side looking out??) the swollen flesh

whose blood is liquid roots
lost searching.
Yet we shall have morethanwings
one unday, swifter than dreams.

Then let us meet by the sea
and walk the breaking waves
with boots of streaming foam
stroll barefoot over treasure
carved of centuries
sun-gilt in an instant!
puppy waves
that rush to lick our
footprints from the shore.

Let us meet in the meadow green
innocent of winter
where soundless shores await our feet
never which returned
as though only lines
we sketched in the sand.

One day we shall speak spring
sweat dew and bleed tiny
flowers, breathe oceans
touch the mist of morning,
but for now
I must be a blind man
guessing at color.

The Climbing Tree

Lord of a timeless little park,
an old familiar ficus giant
overshadows childhood swing sets,
paint chipped and tarnished,
with several decades of colors revealed.

With one root-finger slinking
barely beneath white sand
it holds the first set of swings
steady like a grandfather
while I and my son spider-swing.
Our eyes closed, we imagine flight
high over houses and power lines.

He then begins climbing
the broad tall banyan
suitable for tree tag,
his high up face
the bright and smiling one
among gnarled roots
and dizzy leaf clouds
like the man in the moon.
He craves more height,
scaling branches like years.
I grow terrified, having
long since forgotten the view.
He does not understand
the danger of distance,
unsure foot, nor slight of branch.
Perhaps he trusts the tree.
I keep silent with a strained smile.
Higher he climbs, calling down.

I notice, that from the heights,
he does not stutter now.
Trees are witches and wizards,
bent and crooked, or perhaps green
shaded doorways of another dimension,
somehow, they send down
different children.

Detours Of Good Intent

Self fulfillment
is to gain vision,
yet see nothing.
The clouds are countries
resolved of rulers,
where the buzzard
is a wandering gypsy
sailing the sea of blue
at whose depthless bottom
lay buried stars.
There are universes asleep
in wild grass seed
and wounds are windows
to self awareness,
and I have scaled them,
scaffolds of self-actualization
and kissed truth on the mouth,
but I have forgotten
what it's like
to really hold you...

Healing The Wounded Warrior

Perhaps angels hover near
our slumbering forms,
selecting dreams
the way surgeons
choose scalpels,
to heal us.
Wrestle with me
through the aching darkness.
Then rise and walk with me
into the light of day
where spiders weave in wind
their diamond-threaded dream catchers.

Trails of borrowing worms
break through
the dew-encrusted sand
like varicose veins.
I am careful to step.
In the awareness
of morning
others faults
provide no validation
for my own.
I tell all my wounds
and count my scars.
The healing comes
when I realize
that I have survived
and for this
I have something to give.
The warrior,
the true victor is one
whose defeats become tools.

I have let the burdens
of heavy wounds
bend low my back.
I string now a sinew
of introspect
from toe to head
and I become a bow
shooting forth with shouts
arrows of reclaimed power!

Tokens of our overcoming
we then bind together
within tanned leather
on the heads of proven sticks
to beat the victory drums;
the slain, stretched skins
of personal responsibility.

Together
our sweat falls
as our prayers rise
like steam
from kindled rocks.
Cleansed, free
from the spell of gain
and the toxins
of self-seeking,
we rediscover
the hidden treasures
of friendship.
We are many-
we are one.

Casual Casualties

My bed is a grave
where we consummate
and validate our loneliness,
making love without love,
two soulless bodies.

Propping pillows
against the tombstone,
I sit back and blow
smoke rings
through our hollow silence,
exhaling detachment
as we each die
a little more
inside.

The Ghost Of Imagination

The smell of fresh paint,
new carpet, new house,
the pride of ownership
is a thing of joy. Though,
as a boy, no greater fun had I
than to explore half constructed houses.
I would tunnel forts and cities
in the fresh dirt mounds outside
and the silver slugs
from electrical outlet boxes
were great treasures to be collected.
I would walk through the stud
framework of unpaneled walls
like a spirit, set sail
in loosely placed bathtubs
with my aluminum pipe spyglass.
Rich was my world of quiet imagination.

Now, years later, almost complete,
through my own new house I walk.
Though I would like to think
that some curious lad
christened its rough unfinished floors,
treading wonder and kicking excitement
into its foundations, that he breathed
imagination and curiosity
into the fibers of its walls,
gazed with bright-eyed hope
out its unframed windows
and somewhere,
in some unseen corner
of fresh cement,
left his initials.

The Unseen

Small,
only corners
of light
and sound
spectrums
do we perceive.
Perhaps ideas
actually think
up minds
and flowers
pick people,
knowing all art
silently creates
itself
while seeking
a host
to impregnate,
bearing us
the gift
of last lines,
like bumper stickers
for the mind.

Of Florence Cooper, In Memory

Nothing I remembered
in the bald bright eyed days
when I would squeeze
through doors, fall
through whirling universes dimensionless
two as hands reaching long-
ing to touch themselves
across almost and forever
pulling, loving me through
pain, skin, contracting darkness
throbbing sudden light,
not really doors,
in my new coat of blood
smiling, void of a language
shivering at the whisper
of distant wind
yet not really wind
across the rhythmic soothing sea
the dark thrashing vast
terrible sea, not really sea
twitching, stroking, sucking
with dumb lips
with numb fingers
the shore, the wave-pecked shore
and I shake the snows of Russia
from my wrinkled feet
oh, such a strange dream had I
to awaken
in the photographic timelessness
of daybreak, silent
among the surf-mossy driftwood
a scattered shell
that wind and sea have written on
with the dizzy music
of endless pounding

rushing white, and what matter
if on crampons of burning gold-
en timelessness, upon arches
of silence silver
down scarletary spires of morning
crimson cobalt and cracked dawn day descends
to find my closed eyes
gently with dust
that how asleep I seem
and how that the wind
is once again wind
the sea once again sea, calling
across the darkened cliffs of never
now ablaze with awakening.
Let fall your colorless hair
old woman, newborn babe
of the Infinite I and you
shall live a thousand lives this day
eat breathing stars
as fears become wings
understanding, seeing
when seeing eyes
are only dust.

Autumn

Whispering in tongues of dawn
loneliness on her lips
her changing eyes
full of intensity
she takes me
when I am wild and full
and breaks me bleeds me
that we may share the wine
of each other
in voiceless toast.
Laughing, we run
to where winter cannot
find us
in silence
we share the gift of dance
the wind-dance of dead leaves
naked, unbound and timeless
for we are
the silent winds of seem
hushed with why.
Delicately, slowly
in silence she lets her hair down
turns, lets her eyes
hold summer's warmth
hold the words I cannot speak
and when I've tired
of summer's folly
of too many words
grown sick
of the loud color of day
she gives me barrenness
silence
like a death song
like a cleansing, for she knows
we cannot hide from winter
but only from ourselves.

Conception

From the palm of His hand
my blank soul flutters
blown like star pollen
I cling fast
to the pistol and stamen
of time and space
dipping into forgetfulness
of embryonic fluids
pulling close
chromosome chains
like swaddling cloth
I enter the cocoon
of fetal sleep
letting go of all things
at the whisper
of His command
and begin
the long dark journey
to shape and form.

The Bridge

I waited
at the old wooden bridge,
our Saturday fishing spot,
the same bridge I dove off
to save your ass
when we were young
enough to not be scared
of anything, the bridge
between childhood and manhood.
I waited for you, old friend,
but you never came,
not this Saturday.
So I stood leaning
against the railing
holding a beer
like a lover's hand
while the river closed
its muddy eyes
to unavoidable rocks
and weaved like a dream
beneath the bridge,
the bridge across forever.
I stared down between hands
folded as in prayer, out
over the railing,
but the river would not
talk to me. I thought I knew you,
thought you let me in. I
thought I had all the answers.
The ghost
of the mouth-muffled
gunshot
that echoed across
your empty pasture into mine,
like an arrow, darts by me now

in the startling shot
of a passing car, swift
and unfamiliar, whizzing by
like life itself, leaving me, alone
right in the middle
of the bridge. God
damn you.

The Distant Storms Of Summer

Between hungry earth
and the black
primeval
land of clouds
hovering parallel
angles
a section of rain
liquid thought
transference
spirits
of rivers and seas
cleansed
returning from heaven
and this shall feed
the silent
wisdom
of new grass
bowing
to some distant wind
young and shining
in the hushed glory
of summer.

Blue Mountain Mist Country Inn

There are ghosts
in the kitchen,
aroma spirits
of motherly heritage.
Oh, you could taste
the songs
she sweetly hummed
into the corn hoe cakes
that would spit
and hiss back
in the bacon fat.

Outside, bales of hay
lie in the fields
like dry rolled up tongues
that died
holding their last words.
At night, less shy
curious stars
would come down
to visit us
on the porch swing
flitting about like fairies,
which, really, were fireflies.
I thought
they had all but vanished
with my youth.
Then late,
when everyone else
is asleep,
I lie
in silence
listening
to the night sky
cry over the fields.

As Only Our Eyes See

Black skyscrapers
low on the horizon
like broken teeth
eat the fizzling sun.
I wonder, wander
through crowds, a face
on a corner. Are you one of us—
man in a business suit,
old woman in rags, teenage girl,
strangers in clever disguise?
Our eyes glance-
are you scanning me also,
seeing as only our eyes see,
feeling and sensing pain-
fully deeper,
attuned to the deafening cry
of every rock, tree, the pain
in every face, the fear,
the hopelessness in every eye?

When I move through random streets
cursed of tall clawing concrete
feeling the heartbeat of each building,
the chaos in every cloud,
the tranquil order in each
frenzied pulse of traffic,
every sound screaming volumes
of questions, each moment
a story begging not
to be forgotten, to be told.
I wonder,
has your mind's eye already
been here, has your sixth sense
already probed this random street's
cold fixtures of normality,
felt its way

down this hall of fury and emotion
like a blind sage,
touched its cries of life,
buses, windows, faces, cigarette
butts, sirens, lost smiles,
feeling what they cannot feel,
seeing what they cannot see?
Why us-
cursed with this unrest
of unyielding awareness
which (piercing) reflects back,
separates us, banishes,
condemns us to walk alone.

Fleeing this alien world,
away and alone on some dark beach,
lying back, my thoughts reach up
to caress the moon like a lover.
Are the hands of your mind
silently there, already reaching
from some similar darkness?
Aching, longing, I search faces
on the street,
yet never asking,
"Are you one of us?"
For we must remain silent, secret,
frailest of all creatures,
for to be uncovered, revealed,
rejected,
is to risk death
of the soul. Our forms
clever, diverse, doubtless
in our defenses, our judgments, preconceived ideas,
we could not even spot one another,
lest, at some vulnerable place,
some weak moment,
on the risk of a notion,
we perhaps exchange pleasantries,
"Yes, I too am a poet."

The Accident

On the skid-marked curb
I sit
for a timeless eternity,
groping for my senses
like lost keys,
walk again
the grassy median
pondering images
of my life.
So much
wasted time.
I return again
to the car, still airborne,
sideways above the road,
mangled,
wheels turning
slower than a clock.
I look around me
as though time and life
were but a picture
and yet, I am inside
free to move about.
It is time now..
I hover
over the crumpled hood
reaching down
through twisted metal
and tangled memories
muddled like a kaleidoscope,
shattered glass and
spattered blood
frozen in mid-air,
in blinding white light,
smiling
and take hold
of my wife's
surprised hand...

Until Forever

If I have gone ahead my love,
been buried
like the bulk of a treasure
hidden from the hands
of forgetfulness,
planted like a seed
in the green and tender earth,
know then
that white impatiens are my eyes.
I will watch you.
In the lone cry of an osprey
I will speak your name
at the rising sun.
Raindrops are my fingers
wanting your hair.
The wind rippling field grass
in waves, this is my pulse
racing at the sight of you,
or should the fields be still,
it is my shyness
remembering our first glance
the moment before we danced.
My thoughts are sunlight
calculating down through the cypress trees
visualizing you on the water's edge.
Folded moonlight on new Schefflera leaves,
these are my prayers at night for you.

Walk the shaded boundaries of solitude
where the wind and the Australian pines
become one another
along the beaches where I grew up,
know then
that beyond the other shore,
young again, and tall as fire

I stand poised
to dance across the stars,
ready to choose you
all over again.

Still

I remember Jamaica,
how we moved through the rocks
and the cool rushing water
of Dunn's River Falls,
the way my fingers
explored your sweat-damp hair,
dancers in a misty dream,
the first night of our honeymoon.
How heart hung in my throat
like a smooth stone
morphing into a butterfly
as we parasailed
high above the ocean, as if
I were back, standing at the alter,
watching you walk to me
on your father's arm.

I remember riding horses, bare-back
across the breaking the waves
as though they had wings, and the world
was our singular kingdom, the way I felt
the night we left our reception
hand in hand.

I remember rafting
down a cool mountain stream
where trees along its banks
bowed over the clear water
mixing toxic portions
of light and shadow, as your eyes
through candles over dinner.

I remember warm nights
watching a calm ocean, as though
time's merry-go-round slowed,

almost stopping, with a whole heaven
full of stars, where any dream
were possible. Yes,
I remember Jamaica,
it's in your eyes, still.

After The Fire

Drawn by hollowness
each glance
is a seductive syllable
in the fragmented sentences
of our verbal foreplay.

Yet, when the sparks
of loneliness collide
and ignite the volatile
fuel of passion,
when our separate longings
and hungers combust
and shake the earth,
will we survive lift off
and rocket to new
tender worlds
when the booster fires
of passion subside,
or will we self-destruct,
malfunction, like Challenger?

When you have survived
and outdistanced
the gravitational pull
of my needs,
will you be able
to maintain an orbit
around the world
of my wants?

The Calling Of The Void

Essential
in the guise of molecules vague
visions of ocean calm
desolate storm-scarred shores
summon me
through the surging waves
of timelessness in a dream's waking
asleep breathing rivers
riding the light waves of dawn
an infinity of forevers
hidden in every each now
worlds hidden within worlds
scattered like dust
sweating distance beyond mind
my feet burn to touch them
strange sands
ghostly rivers of whenlessness
alternate philosophies
born of a moon-hushed quiet
of alien skies
a terse to-do of odd trees ablaze
with stillness, silence of twilight
air of thing, worlds hung upon nothing
like thoughts in a mind
ifs of dream, nows of never
trying and retrying themselves, dewdrops
each second holding infinite universes
what supple destinies
thread the horizons of such
weaving the untouchable
fabric of seemishness
dancing upon crystal
towers of dreams.

Who would venture the straights of time
brave the black worm hole dimensionless void
to live a sunrise's moment
alone assume eternity
to hold stars in their hand
empty space
enters you
and you die, drift gently
drifting petals
on silver rivers of nowhere
that touch the frightened shores
of believing
until what morning draws us
from death's dark tunnel
and we tell our dreams-
leafish bodies on wings of wind...

Surtsey
(The Island of)

Under primeval skies you rose
from the ocean's icy depths
like the molten fiery ghost
of Atlantis
weary seagulls
the only citizens
of your black beaches
that yield to fields
made of ground rainbows
of sulfur
edging the jagged
spaces of lavascape
like an alien moon
while the earth still heaves
and trembles still
from your violent birth
rudely belching steam.

Angrily the ocean devours
with frothy spider arms
what it has bore
as you struggle
to justify your existence
with sea rocket and lyme grass
all the while the traitor currents
baring seed in secret
the lost bounty
of mermaid's purses.

Surtsey, sanctuary
of the spirit of newness
you mirror the origin
of all things
yet your young banks
will grow steep with soon
as from the shores of time
you will disappear
when the relentless waves
have their way
and again
stone gives way to water.

Epitaph In Storm

Lightening cracked the black sky
broke open the winds
reaching up through the clouds
the souls
of those born into the dust
climbed sharp raindrops
into the gentle blue
hereafter
I shall, on concepts
far above language
of time and space
leave but of myself
a faint
indistinct
shadow upon the ground
and returning use sparingly
the crystal clearness
of raindrops
fearing their paradoxical
dark gathering
for too much clearness
becomes a frightening
thundering blackness
against the naked light of day.

Sunset Serenity

Concede not
to the taskmaster worry
toiling over straw
bricks of detail
for today is the yesterday
that stands powerless tomorrow
but walk with me
in Seminole mind
as the ripe evening sun
slips behind a small distance
of melaleucas trees
setting fire
to their silhouettes
watch with me
as thousands
upon thousands
of tree swallows
gather over the Everglades
like a giant soot cloud
a black shifting sea
of integrated movement
then descend
like a tornado
emptying
one after another
a swerving funnel cloud
slowly sucked
into an endless
sea of saw grass
a million demons
descending into Hell
as the last impulse of day
changes its mind I think
as birds
angels enter

the earth's atmosphere
drifting down breathless heights
soundless reaches
above the haste
circling, contemplating
the souls of men
knowing
he who dies
with no regrets
hath lived in victory.

Florida

Small flocks
of various hopes, dreams
from all across the city
converge at sunset
to fly away,
out over the Everglades
beyond the horizon
disappearing into the
clouds like angels
who become waitresses
while the shrouded sun
a drunken stagehand
behind the painted
cardboard clouds
fumbles the lighting
to sudden
glorious white gold-
en majesty
beyond all fear
then slowly settles
to the earth
like a regret
melting into the anonymity
of sawgrass
great Australian pines (the wind
through whose bodies becomes
the very breath
of imagination) fierce
bent old men
that rage out
from canal banks
where needled ripples
dispel the reflected illusions
of life
and north, from above

the orange grove rippled hills
folds of plush
green corduroy seem
to stretch on forever
like summer
nights on the beach
with the full moon rising
like a burning ship
against the horizon
lured, quenched
by the ancient
timeless tune
of the tranquil waves.

Youth And Age

Walking the rails
along the railroad tracks,
my two sons and I,
the rebelliousness of youth
and the conformity of age,
we reach out
across the oil-stained granite rocks
between the splintered ties
to try and touch hands
without losing our balance.

How they need my direction,
my foresight, and I,
the unclouded purity,
the honest questioning heart
beneath their actions.

The late morning sun
is silver diamond dust
glistening off the rails
while all of life is an adventure
despite the inevitable
unseen train,
the unspoken fear,
so deliciously frightening.

Suddenly, up ahead- something dead!
We jump down off the rails and run
with our hearts pounding
like locomotives driven,
they by the soon to be shattered
innocence of curiosity, and I
by the protective instinct of love.

In the middle of the tracks
we meet
for a moment,
the tender soul of youth,
the hard closed heart of age
prisoner of rationalization,
and stand in flooded silence,
they with deep questions and concerns
and I with the horror of decay
at the weather-beaten
scantly fur clad skeleton
of a dog.

I cannot cover their eyes to life,
but only hold their hand.

Touched, different, somehow
older, we mount our separate tracks
to cross the great trestle up ahead.
Silent, the wild sky above us,
beneath us, the raging
river running soft.

Half across
I pause a daydream glance
down the backyard banks
and on ahead
into the disappearing distance
to where, it seems,
the two tracks meet.

In Memory Of Tomorrow

Wind ideas
idly stir the trees
sucking the tender pink
of twilight
evening
lets fall
from dark fingers
the toy-like sun
daring to touch the white
chasteness of skyscrapers
touch them soft
with quivering shadows
ah, but morning's touch be softer
for she handles newborn
flowers
touching deep
as time
who will mark his path
with fallen suns
and press his wine
from unclaimed dreams
the wine of maybe
until we stand on eternity
and turn
one last look
on Earth
in all her faded glory
realizing
we were in paradise all along.

Not Yet

Morning speaks in mist to Istanbul.
The cobbled streets respond, echo
with peddler's cries and the bustling of hamals
down ancient streets too narrow for trucks,
their backs bent over, heavy laden with wares.
Bright-eyed little peasants clutching coins
scurry to the shouts of hot sesame-encrusted simit.
Boyacis make ready for work their brass
elaborately carved shoeshine boxes handed down
from generations past, they do not notice me.
With my feet in shoes of death
I walk the dawn- disembodied, relative.
I am the morning
luring the earth awake with wonder,
actuating, fostering, losing myself in day.
I am a leaf now, painted with autumn,
stolen by the wind, my wild lover.
I waver. I flutter. I glide.
Exhausted, in bliss I touch ground.
Now I am a new blade of grass
poking out my green tender head,
struggling free from dark earth,
small, insignificant, indifferent.
A passing dog lifts one leg
to shower me in its arrogance,
I do not care. I am the sun now,
deep in some dusty sky.
I grow weary. I grow old.
I walk the streets of Paris at night
with too much wine on my breath.
A tattered and tainted overcoat
conceals my tired wings of gold.
I stoop beneath a street lamp,
read the trampled poetry
chalked on the sidewalk,

place my coin in the square. Apathetic,
I play the senseless game of forever.
I move on now.
You cannot follow,
not here,
not yet...

Tears

She stands slender like a flower
awaiting the wind's justice
in some morning soft mist
that now hangs heavily upon her,
as does certain woe.
Her rosy cheeks
host sorrow's untimely dew
that she cannot resist,
tears, the child
of ten thousand things perhaps,
I do not know.
Does she weep at death's swiftness,
fate, or perhaps an impetuous boy,
or perhaps she feels the pain
of too much tenderness,
too much joy.

The Waiting Wind

The wind is an old man
who teaches the trees
to dance, or perhaps
the wind is a child,
the yet unspeaking babe
of silence,
silence yet to come,
a sensual lover
sipping of ocean
as though it were wine
kissing then suddenly
gently, my lips.

On summer lazy days
it becomes the music
of my idleness,
the breath of the earth,
the electrifying
forceful wind,
the gentle yielding wind.

Perhaps the wind
is the dusty voice
of the dead,
whispering
from the other side
of forever,
waiting
once more
for their children
to be born.

The Breath Of Enlightenment

The spirit sends visions
through the mind's blind spots,
hieroglyphic dreams
from the inner walls of the soul
pre-dating words,
that only the journeying heart
can decipher in stillness,
breathing the steps
of its stepless journey,
guided by sea sounds,
mother of all music.
Unleashed spirit
and healed heart
fuse in body
when we become as the shore,
accepting the tide
and the molding of the waves,
hidden tide pools,
faceless and free
in our own identify.

To be alone
and to dance,
to pass words
among friends
like wine
and together
break the bread
of ideas.

Spring

Timeless,
I know you(me)now,
I can feel you inside me
touchless, your green
searching fingers.
Coalesce with me, absorb me
lose me in your
omnipotent spontaneity.
My ear sunward, below
the dusty scratching roots
I heard the thunder
of thousand voices- rain
as you ran through(me)the fields.
Silent, with dirt in my eyes
from beneath
the stretched bloody roots
I watched you
raise your hand
across burning meadows
heard stamens
whisper to thistledown, "nnnow..."
I felt mountains breathe,
yet your voice
half robin/half wind
half silence
could not find my ears
for the flowers
you held bleeding
freshly picked at your side,
I heard only their screams.

The Analogous Birds

An alien in the meadow,
my clumsy steps scatter birds
like a handful of pebbles
thrown to the wind
by a child,
migratory birds,
travelers of forever.
Each journey's end
is but another's beginning,
each answer
another question.
The wild southlands,
the harsh changing northlands
render home
for but a season's brief
thus migration,
secret sweet lust
for the rash
uncertainty of wandering,
the beauty of endless
directionless flight,
effortless motion-
less, steep
on the lofty winds,
frailties of feather
touchless,
defeating invisible
adversaries of current,
proclaiming sovereignty
of the clouds...
but I can walk now,
contented,
for I have touched the white
unfolded wings of wonder.

Acknowledgements

Firewood, Eternity & The Breath Of Enlightenment- were first published by Cosmic Trend of Canada in "Lighter Than Light"

Silent Reaches & The Measure Of Distance- were first published by Byline Magazine

Cafe Gypsies, Healing The Wounded Warrior & The Analogous Birds- were first published by Cosmic Trend of Canada in "Birds And Angels"

The Hands Of Time, Lost Oceans, Silent Touch & Surtsey- were first published by Cosmic Trend of Canada in "Infinitely Whispering Surfs"

The Fountain & Listen- were first published by Cosmic Trend of Canada in "Beyond Dimensions Of Truth"

Echoes In The Wind- was first published by East Coast Academy of Poets in "Poetry In The Woods 5th Anthology"

Discovery, Life Cycle, Ghost Crossing, Trophies Of Ego, The Unseen & Conception- were first published by Cosmic Trend of Canada in "PARA*phrase Newsletter"

Free Fall, Fallen Blossoms & Until Forever- were first published by Cosmic Trend of Canada in "And I Will Slay All Your Dragons"

Echoes Of Destiny, The Braille Brief And Beyond, The Accident & Epitaph In Storm- were first published by Cosmic Trend of Canada in "Tornados Of Calm"

Detours Of Good Intent & As Only Our Eyes See- were first published by Cosmic Trend of Canada in "Private Crystallography"

Casual Casualties & Autumn- were first published by Cosmic Trend of Canada in "Bottomless Chalice"

Of Florence Cooper, In Memory- was first published by Cosmic Trend of Canada in "Dragon Flowers"

The Distant Storms Of Summer, In Memory Of Tomorrow & Spring- were first published by Cosmic Trend of Canada in "Seasons Of The Flow"

Still- was first published by Cosmic Trend of Canada in "Future Memories"

After The Fire- was first published by Cosmic Trend of Canada in "From The First Drop"

The Calling Of The Void- was first published by Cosmic Trend of Canada in "Forgotten Alien Skies"

Florida- was first published by Cosmic Trend of Canada in "Tomorrows Seem Forever"

The Waiting Wind- was first published by The International Library of Poetry in "America At The Millennium"

Biography

Though an eager traveler, Chuck Rice still lives content where he grew up, in Fort Lauderdale, Florida with his beautiful wife, having been blessed with four sons and two grandchildren. The adventures of the outdoors; hiking and exploring, are some of his passions. Chuck's poetry has been published by Florida Atlantic University, Iowa State University and Byline Magazine, in addition to appearing in many anthologies published by Cosmic Trend of Canada, with whom Chuck previously published one chapbook of poetry, entitled "And I Will Slay All Your Dragons".